Employee Engagement 2.0

How to Motivate Your Team for High Performance

A Real-World Guide for Busy Managers

Sixth Edition

New York Times Bestselling Author
Inc 500 – Best Place To Work Winner

Kevin Kruse

www.KevinKruse.com

Want to quickly generate massive loyalty and extra effort among all your team members?

This is your step-by-step guide that will teach you:

- What employee engagement is (it does not mean happy or satisfied)
- How engagement directly drives sales, profits, and even stock price
- The secret recipe for making anyone feel engaged
- How to quantify engagement, even if you have no budget
- 7 questions to ask that will identify your engagement weakness
- What to say to facilitate a team meeting on engagement
- A communication system that ensures rapid, two-way flow of information
- How to make your strategic vision memorable and "sticky"
- How to implement a complete engagement plan in only 8 weeks!

Copyright © 2012-2016 by Kevin Kruse
All rights reserved. No part of this publication may be reproduced, stored in a retrieval system, or transmitted by any means – electronic, mechanical, photographic (photocopying), recording, or otherwise – without prior permission in writing from the author.
Published in Richboro, PA, by The Kruse Group.
ISBN-13: 978-1469996134
ISBN-10: 1469996138
First printing: 2012

FREE ONLINE QUIZ
DISCOVER YOUR ENGAGEMENT STYLE

As a special gift for readers of this book you can access a complimentary online version of The Personal Engagement Profile. It will reveal your current level of engagement and will provide a thorough analysis of the triggers that make *you* feel fully engaged at work.

Launch Quiz: www.KevinKruse.com/profile

Bulk Purchases and Speaking

For information on discounts for bulk purchases, or to invite Kevin to speak at your next event, call The Kruse Group at: 267-756-7089 or e-mail info@kevinkruse.com.

Table of Contents

PREFACE:
NOT YOUR TYPICAL
BUSINESS BOOK

OK, I know you're not reading this book for fun. You aren't learning about "employee engagement" sitting in a beach chair just for kicks (um, you aren't, are you?).

Either you were told to read this book by someone at your company, or you are sick and tired of your apathetic team and are hoping this book can help you to shake some life into them. The good news is that while I can't say this is as fun as a Stephen King novel, it won't be painful.

I'm neither an Ivy League professor nor a Human Resources expert. I don't do mumbo-jumbo or academic theory. Just real-world stuff that I've used myself.

You see, I've started and sold several businesses and I've won a lot of awards over the years, but the only one I'm actually a little proud of is the **Best Place to Work** in

Pennsylvania award. It was based on anonymous surveys of workers throughout the state. When your own troops say you're doing a good job, it feels pretty good

Furthermore, I've learned that not only can engagement lead to amazing business results; it can also have a tremendous impact on people's lives, too. Our emotions at work carry over to our personal lives, and being dissatisfied or stressed at work can lead to problems with our health, our marriages, and even with our children.

Fortunately, creating engaged teams doesn't require a lot of time or money. I never had the luxury of a big HR department or an outside consultant.

If I can do it, you can, too. This quick read will set you on your way.

Introduction: Remember Flight Attendant, Steven Slater?

Steven Slater. Remember the name?

It was August 9, 2010 when JetBlue flight attendant, Steven Slater, decided to quit his job in spectacular fashion.

After having some kind of altercation with a passenger, upon landing Slater cursed everyone out over the PA system, grabbed two beers, deployed the inflatable emergency slide, and slid down to freedom.

What's amazing isn't the crazy incident itself, but rather what happened afterward.

Within 24 hours Steven Slater dominated the news. "Felon or working class hero?" screamed the headlines. He topped Twitter trends and his Facebook page quickly gained 182,000 fans. Late night talk show host, Jay Leno, filled a monologue with Slater jokes:

- *"The pilots were furious. That was their last two beers."*

- *"The good news is that terrorists are now scared to fly JetBlue."*

- *"JetBlue has a new slogan: Screw all of you!"*

Clearly, the Steven Slater incident touched a nerve of popular culture. It's as if everyone—not just HR professionals and organizational experts—understood that people everywhere are unhappy and stressed out at work. It was an interesting and somewhat amusing anecdote that made accessible these boring and bleak statistics.

Only 34% of employees are engaged at work.
(source: Gallup 2016)

Only 48% of workers are *satisfied* with their job, according to a 2015 survey by The Conference Board.

Indeed, **job satisfaction is near an all-time low**.

And this is where you come in. *If you care*, you can drive higher levels of engagement. But you *do* have to care.

CHAPTER 1: WHAT IS EMPLOYEE ENGAGEMENT, ANYWAY?

OK, first things first. What the heck is "employee engagement" anyway?

Let's first talk about what it's *not*.

Engaged doesn't mean happy. Someone might be happy at work, but that doesn't mean they're productive. In fact, we all probably know "Happy Joe" who's always humming a tune, chatting at the copy machine, volunteering to make the lunch run. We wonder, doesn't that guy have any work to do?

Engaged doesn't mean satisfied. This is a big misconception. So many companies have "employee satisfaction" surveys. Being "satisfied" is a good start, but it doesn't go far enough. Someone can be satisfied at work,

5

but only satisfied enough to be a clock-watching nine-to-fiver. They can be satisfied, but will still take the call from the recruiter who is promising them a 5% bump in pay. Satisfied isn't enough.

Here is the definition of engagement:

Employee engagement is the emotional commitment an employee has to the organization and its goals.

Engaged employees actually *care* about their work. They aren't doing it because they have to, or just for the paycheck, or even just to get a promotion.

When employees care—when they are *engaged*—they use **discretionary effort**, they go the extra mile. It means:

- An engaged salesperson will sell just as hard on Friday afternoon as she does on Monday morning

- An engaged customer service representative will try just as hard to delight a customer at 5:00 PM as she does at 10:00 AM

- An engaged software engineer will leave code cleaner than when she was given it

- Engaged factory workers will have fewer accidents and be more productive

The 10:6:2 Rule states that every 10% improvement in commitment increases employee effort by 6%, and every 6% increase in effort increases performance by 2% (source: Corporate Executive Board).

In addition to discretionary effort, engaged employees stay in your company longer; they are less likely to be lured away by the siren song of head hunters.

The 10:9 Rule states that every 10% improvement in commitment decreases an employee's probability of departure by 9% (source: Corporate Executive Board).

Now you can begin to see how an engaged employee is different than just a happy or satisfied employee. Now let's see why engagement is so important to businesses.

CHAPTER 2: YES, ENGAGEMENT DRIVES GROWTH AND PROFITS

You hear CEOs say all the time, "People are our most important asset." But most of the time they really don't mean it.

If we could be a fly on the wall in the executive board room do you think we'd hear more talk about sales or recruiting? About profit levels or retention rates? Stock price or morale?

I think we all know the answers.

Above all else, C-level executives are trying to increase shareholder value. Right or wrong, they care more about investor returns than anything else.

The good news is that **employee engagement is the secret ingredient that actually leads to a higher stock**

price. If you need to convince yourself, or convince your boss, about the value of employee engagement just focus on these research findings:

- The most **engaged companies had five times higher total shareholder return** over five years, compared to the least engaged companies, in a 2009 study conducted by Kenexa.

- **Engaged companies have 6% higher net profit margins**, according to a Towers Perrin 2011 study.

- According to Gallup, the retail chain, B&Q, gained an extra £70 million a year to its sales from increased engagement.

Why does employee engagement lead to hard return-on-investment results? How does it work?

The answer is what I call the **Engagement-Shareholder Value Chain**, which is an expanded form of the Service-Profit Chain first described by James Heskett and Earl Sasser.

Remember that engaged employees care more and work harder. Now imagine a series of dominos that trigger each other in a chain:

Engaged Employees → Work Harder, Longer, with More Focus → Increases Productivity, Increases Service, Increases Quality → More Satisfied Customers → More Sales, More Profit → Higher Stock Share Price → Higher Total Shareholder Value

In addition, companies with engaged employees have reduced costs because fewer employees leave. That means lower recruiting costs, lower training and on-boarding costs, too.

Making sense?

A simpler way to think about it is this:

Culture always trumps strategy.

In other words, you can have the best strategy in the world, but if nobody cares it isn't going to matter.

And the converse is true. I often had the wrong strategy, but because I had great people working in a great culture, they figured it out. They wouldn't let me get in their way.

We started this chapter with CEOs who truly don't get it. But they aren't all that way. In fact, there was one CEO who proved the value of employee engagement in dramatic fashion.

CASE STUDY: The Campbell Soup Company

Once upon a time, in the year 2000, the Campbell Soup Company was in big trouble.

The company that began in 1869 and sold soup in 120 countries hit a wall. Sales weren't just slowing, they were declining. Campbell lost 54% of their market value in just one year. Campbell's executives were told that their employee engagement levels were the worst ever seen among the Fortune 500.

So the board of directors hired a new CEO, the mild-mannered Douglas Conant, to turn things around.

What do most CEOs do in dire situations?

They might sell off divisions, buy smaller competitors, move into new markets, or maybe even hire investment bankers to evaluate "strategic options."

But that wasn't Doug Conant's style. A *Forbes* magazine article quoted him as saying:

"To win in the marketplace ... you must first win in the workplace. I'm obsessed with keeping employee engagement front and center."

So quarter after quarter, year after year, Conant made sure that employee engagement was one of the top initiatives for the Campbell Soup Company.

By 2009, the ratio of engaged employees to disengaged employees reached an astounding **23-to-1**.

More importantly, in the decade that saw the S&P 500 stocks lose 10% of their value, Campbell's stock actually increased by 30%.

In other words, "keeping employee engagement front and center" helped Campbell to achieve **four times greater results for investors**.

For more research that shows the correlation between employee engagement and business results see the Appendix.

CHAPTER 3:
IMPROVE YOUR
HEALTH, KIDS AND
SEX LIFE (OH MY!)

Did you know that people who are dissatisfied with their jobs are far more likely to be hospitalized or even die from a heart attack or other cardiac event? That's the conclusion of the famous Swedish WOLF study that tracked over 3,000 men over a decade.

Did you know that if a parent has a bad day at work, his/her child is more likely to misbehave in school the next day? This was the conclusion of a 1996 Queen's University study that had fathers fill out daily questionnaires about work stress, and teachers fill out surveys about their kids' behaviors.

In a 1985 NYU study of 500 married couples, they found a direct correlation between job satisfaction and marital intimacy. In other words, if you come home after a bad day at work, your spouse will match your mood, and you can't expect much "intimacy" later that night.

How can this be? How can our jobs impact our physical health, our kids and our relationships?

Psychologists call this the spillover and crossover effects. Your emotions at work—good or bad—spill over into your personal life, *and even cross over to those around you.*

You don't need to be a psychologist to know this is true. If you come home from work in a good mood, you might kiss your spouse hello, make dinner together, and share the day's events over a couple glasses of wine. That's a night with some possibility!

DEFINITIONS

Spillover effect: the positive or negative effects of an individual's working life on their personal life.

Crossover effect: the transfer of positive or negative emotions from an individual to their spouse, or to other family members.

What about on a bad day? You might come home and grunt hello as you flip through the junk mail. Grab a beer and plunk down in front of the TV tuned to junk. That's probably a night that won't have a lot to offer.

It's the same with our role as a parent. Come home happy and we're more likely to play with our kids, praise them, or help them with their homework. Come home grumpy and we shoo them away or snap at them. Children internalize rejection and punishment and express it as either withdrawal or acting out.

So, why should you care about all this? Isn't this book supposed to be about practical real-world steps to leading engaged teams? Well, it turns out this is the most important chapter of the book.

Want better health?
Become fully engaged at work.

Want a better marriage?
Become fully engaged at work.

Want to be happy in life?
Become fully engaged at work.

To lead, you have to care. You can't fake it.

You have to understand—to really know—that your behavior as a boss impacts your team members' health, marriages and even their kids.

I'm going to tell you exactly *how* to drive engagement in a few more pages. But more important is the *why* of engagement. All those business benefits in the previous chapter are true, and those are good *logical* reasons you should care about engagement. But logical reasons fade away in the face of never ending to-do lists, overlapping meetings, and oh so many tasks.

You need to soak in this chapter so that when you see your team members—when you pass them in the hall, sit with them at lunch, meet in the conference room, whenever you see their faces—you also see their spouses, their children, and realize the influence you have on their personal lives.

CHAPTER 4:
THE SECRET
RECIPE FOR
MAKING PEOPLE
FEEL "ENGAGED"

OK. Now we're ready to dig in. We know what engagement is, how it drives amazing business results, and the surprising ways that it affects people's personal lives.

But what makes someone *feel* engaged? It *is* a feeling. So how do we get people to feel the feeling of engagement?

Gallup research indicates that 70% of the variance in engagement comes from one's relationship with her boss. As the saying goes, "People join companies but leave bosses." This is an important point worth repeating.

Whether someone feels engaged at work or not is usually based on their relationship with their direct superior.

This means you need to take responsibility, as a manager, for the engagement of your team. Sure there are all kinds of external factors out of your control. The CEO doesn't have a crisp vision, the new product launch is delayed, and the computers are old and the software outdated, the food in the cafeteria stinks, whatever.

People join companies, but they leave their boss.

But I've seen over and over again that within the same company, some teams have high levels of engagement and others have low levels of engagement. They all have the same CEO, the same tools, the same cafeteria. What's different is their manager.

You **are responsible for the engagement of your team.** Don't look elsewhere.

The good news is that you can do this. Leading for engagement isn't an inherent trait or highly developed skill. If you do and say the things I'll teach in the chapters ahead, you will increase engagement.

It's true that there is no one universal model for what drives engagement. A simple Google search will yield different answers from esteemed companies like Kenexa, Hay Group and Gallup.

Also, most of those models are complex. Maybe because they truly need to be; maybe because if it's complex you'll need to hire their experts to figure it out.

Based on my own experience leading "Best Place to Work" teams, and my analysis of the available research I believe that it can be boiled down to four things.

Communication. Do your team members feel that there is frequent, consistent *two-way* communication?

Growth and Development. Do your team members feel like they are learning new things and advancing their career?

Recognition & Appreciation. Do your team members feel appreciated and that their ideas count?

Trust & Confidence. Do your team members trust the leadership and have confidence in the organization's future?

To help you remember these key drivers, remember the phrase, "Communicate GReAT." With GReAT being an acronym for Growth, Recognition, And Trust.

REMEMBER IT!

Use this handy phrase and acronym to remember the four key drivers of engagement.

Communicate GReAT!

Great leaders **Communicate**
Growth, **R**ecognition, **A**nd **T**rust

If this is starting to sound complicated, don't fear. There are only two main points in this chapter.

First, you—as manager—are the one who can most influence engagement.

Second, the things you can do to drive engagement—which don't require a lot of time or money—are:

- **Communication**
- **Growth**
- **Recognition**
- **and Trust**

Now let's break down step by step how you can trigger those drivers to increase engagement.

CHAPTER 5: WHAT'S YOUR PERSONAL ENGAGEMENT STYLE?

Individuals have different preferences, or triggers, for feeling engaged at work. Younger workers might be more driven by growth than older workers. Some people might want more recognition than others. It's important for you as a manager to get to know each of your direct reports so you tailor your leadership support, but it's also important *to understand your own preferences*, which may be influencing your leadership style.

For example, I know that I'm a growth junkie. What really gets me engaged is when I've got a big challenge, I'm learning new things, and developing in new ways. Recognition is nice, but I don't actually care about it that much, and public praise makes me squirm.

So how do you think I come off as a manager?

Well, my natural reflex is to talk to my team members about growth. *Hey, what area do you want to develop in this year? Hey, do you want to go to that cool conference? Hey, here's a copy of a book I just read that I think you'll enjoy.* Growth, growth, growth.

How often do I pull the "recognition" trigger? Not as often as I should. I'm quick with a polite thank you all the time, but I'm horrible at recognizing people in public, I keep forgetting to send out thank you notes, and I absolutely hate doing awards.

But because I know this about myself, I can adjust. I can make sure to be more mindful of recognition actions if I want to engage my team members.

To help you to identify your own engagement preferences—your natural style—I've developed a short profile. You can complete the profile online to get a nifty score and bar chart summary, or you can just manually answer the questions and do the math below.

Discover Your Personal Engagement Profile

To complete your profile, visit
www.kevinkruse.com/profile

To complete the profile manually, consider each statement below and reflect on how much you agree or disagree with its sentiment. Write the number that most closely matches your level of agreement. Remember this scale:

1 = "Strongly Disagree"

2 = "Disagree"

3 = "Neutral"

4 = "Agree"

5 = "Strongly Agree"

COMMUNICATION

_____ Meeting with my manager one-on-one, at least weekly, is extremely important to me.

_____ Meeting with my fellow teammates, at least weekly, is extremely important to me.

_____ Reading company-wide communications, like the annual report or company newsletters is extremely important to me.

_____ Being able to ask questions of company leadership is extremely important to me.

GROWTH

_____ Career advancement is extremely important to me.

_____ I need to be challenged at work.

_____ Having a mentor to help guide my career is extremely important to me.

_____ Knowing the next steps in my career path is extremely important to me.

RECOGNITION

_____ Having a manager who says thank you, when appropriate, is extremely important to me.

_____ Having team members who say thank you is extremely important to me.

_____ I feel really good when one of my ideas is implemented at work.

_____ I need my opinions at work to be considered seriously.

TRUST

_____ Knowing my company's goals is extremely important to me.

_____ I need to know how my work contributes to my company's goals.

_____ It is extremely important to have a manager who cares about me.

_____ It is extremely important that our senior leaders do what they say they will do.

Calculate Your Engagement Style

Add up your scores for the first four questions under the Communication heading, and write the total next to the word "COMMUNICATION" below.

Add up your scores for the second set of questions under the Growth heading, and write the total next to the word "GROWTH" below.

Add up your scores for the third set of questions under the Recognition heading, and write the total next to the word "RECOGNITION" below.

Add up your scores for the final set of four questions under the Trust heading, and write the total next to the word "TRUST" below.

_____   COMMUNICATION

_____   GROWTH

_____   RECOGNITION

_____   TRUST

Interpreting Your Scores

Which engagement driver received your highest score? Circle it above, or write it on a Post-it note and stick it on your computer monitor. This driver is your primary key for unlocking feelings of engagement at work. This is the #1 area for you—and your manager—to focus on in your career.

Do you have a tie, or are several scores close? Each engagement driver can have a score ranging from 4 to 20.

Many people have two or more engagement triggers that are tied or several that are just within a point or two of each other. If this is the case for you, consider it a good thing. It means that there is more than one way to trigger your feelings of engagement.

Consider these items to be tools in your engagement toolbox. If one of the four drivers scored much higher than the others, then you want to look for nails to use with that "hammer." But if you have several drivers that scored high, that means you have a hammer, a screwdriver, and a wrench in your engagement toolbox and you'll have many more opportunities to trigger engagement.

Are all your scores 12 or below? If all the drivers have a score of 12 or less, it means that you answered every single question as neutral or with a level of disagreement. You are basically indicating that communication, growth, recognition, and trust aren't important to you. Although this result is very rare, there are other drivers of engagement that turn up less frequently, including teamwork, quality, and corporate responsibility. You should reflect on these items, and any others you can think of, to identify your own engagement triggers.

Now, let's get back to a step-by-step plan for increasing your team's engagement.

CHAPTER 6:
STEP ONE,
MEASURE IT

If you want something to improve you need to measure it. This is true of employee engagement, too.

Now, if your company is already running an annual engagement survey and you're getting a report on how your team is doing, that's great. Just skip th is chapter.

But let's assume you have no idea of the current engagement level of your team. Having a feeling about it doesn't count. You need a number. You need a specific number that you can then look back on to see if your engagement efforts are working or not.

In every one of my companies I would do an engagement check every six months.

Most companies either don't measure engagement at all, or they do a survey every two years. The big consulting companies will tell you to do one every year. I don't think that's enough.

The problem with doing them annually, or (Heaven forbid) every two years, is that factors outside of your control might impact the scores a bit (while you, as a boss, are the primary driver, you aren't the *only* driver).

For example, if you do an engagement survey after laying off 20% of your company, that would negatively impact your scores. If you do an engagement check right after launching a major new product, or issuing big bonus checks, that might skew the scores in the positive. It's not that those results would be invalid; it's just that you don't know if they are lasting. Thus, doing an engagement check every six months ensures that you see the big picture and nuances of the external events are smoothed out.

When it comes to actually measuring your team's level of engagement you have three options.

OPTION 1:
HIRE AN ENGAGMENT RESEARCH COMPANY

If you are a senior executive with a large extended team (say 100 people or more) and a decent budget, the right way to measure engagement is to hire an external company to administer an employee engagement survey.

Hiring outside experts means you'll get a tailored set of survey questions, detailed analysis including question correlations, and you'll be able to benchmark your own organization against their other clients in the database.

If you need recommendations for a companies that do this kind of work just email me at info@kevinkruse.com.

OPTION 2:
DO YOUR OWN QUICK AND DIRTY SURVEY

Survey experts and HR professionals would tell you doing your own survey is crazy; leave it to experts. They'll tell you all the reasons why a "do-it yourself" approach is flawed. But I say, if you can't afford to hire outside experts, doing it yourself is better than nothing.

To administer your own survey, you'll want to sign-up for an online survey service like SurveyMonkey (http://www.surveymonkey.com). You can get basic services for free, or pay a little and get more functionality.

Using an online survey program will enable you to create the survey, send it out to your team members, and to easily calculate the scores.

When you go to create your survey, you'll want to choose your question type. All questions will be a standard "Likert-scale" which means you are asking if people agree or disagree, using a five point scale.

1. Strongly Disagree
2. Disagree
3. Neutral
4. Agree
5. Strongly Agree

Now come the questions themselves. There are just seven of them:

1. I am extremely satisfied working in [company name].
2. I rarely think about finding a new job in a different company.
3. I would recommend [company name] to my friends as a great place to work.
4. There is frequent, two-way communication at [company name].
5. [Company name] provides me with sufficient opportunities for learning and development.
6. I feel appreciated at work.
7. I am confident that [company name] has a bright future.

The first three questions measure current levels of engagement using methodology similar to how you would measure customer satisfaction. In fact, if you want an approximate level of a person's engagement level, you could average the scores for question 1, 2 and 3. Similarly, if you want to see the overall engagement of your team, department or company, you could average the scores for these questions for everyone in the group.

The next four questions measure the key drivers of engagement (i.e., communication, growth, recognition and trust).

You should send out the survey and give people two weeks to complete it.

More time won't really increase the response rate, and less time means you might miss people who have taken a week's vacation. Make sure to remind people to take it if they haven't done so, and explain that you really do care about their results, and will share the results with the whole team.

To score the survey when it's complete, just run a summary report which will give you the average score for each question.

So, what's a good score?

In general, using a five point rating system, you should consider scores above 4.0 to be very good, between 3.5 and 4.0 as good, and anything below a 3.5 as bad.

I won a Best Place to Work in PA award with overall engagement scores around 4.2. One accomplished survey researcher told me, *"The rule of thumb is, 4's are great and if you see 2's you're going to start seeing people quit."*

The biggest problems with doing your own surveys are the issues of confidentiality and anonymity. Surveys should be confidential to get honest feedback, and using an outside survey company gives confidence to your employees that indeed it will be anonymous.

But when you do your own survey, even if you set it up to be anonymous, employees will rightly wonder if there isn't some way you'll be tracking their responses back to their individual email or IP addresses.

There is no solution to this other than to tell your team that the survey is anonymous, and that you are just going to be looking at the average scores for each question to see how you can do a better job as a leader. It might help if the survey software is actually setup and utilized by an administrative assistant or even someone in another department.

OPTION 3:
DO A "STAY INTERVIEW" (i.e., JUST HAVE A CONVERSATION ABOUT IT)

If you have a really small team, say less than five people, doing a web-based survey might not be practical, and it becomes far harder to ensure anonymity. In this case,

I suggest you just have a good old fashion conversation with your team.

This approach is also known as a "stay interview." Many are familiar with the concept of exit interviews—interviews conducted by HR when someone resigns to discuss what led to the departure. A stay interview is similar, but is designed to find out what will make someone stay in the company.

A recent issue of *HR Magazine* (December 2011) shared the case of Burcham Hills Retirement Community which decreased turnover by 72% by implementing annual stay interviews with all veteran employees.

Stay interviews reduced turnover by 72% in one company.

The idea is to literally ask your team members about their current levels of engagement and how they feel about the issues of Communication, Growth, Recognition and Trust. You shouldn't just hammer them with the verbatim questions while taking notes. Make it more conversational.

Also, this initial conversation is more about understanding their current perceptions about how things are going. You don't have to get into solving the problems (we'll do that later).

For example, when I took over leadership of a small four person non-profit, one of the first things I did was have one-on-one conversations and I asked them how they were feeling about things. I needed to know whether they were gung ho and fired up, or if they going to hand me a resignation letter within a few days. An "engagement conversation" should be conversational. For example, let's assume a manager is talking to a direct-report named Amanda...

Manager: So, Amanda, it's really important to me that we're all engaged at work and I want to really focus on our team's engagement moving forward. Can you tell me how things have been going for you...how satisfied are you with your job lately?

Amanda: Things are OK. You know, some days are better than others.

Manager: Well it sounds like you're pretty satisfied, but you aren't jumping out of bed each morning thrilled to be heading into work. Do you think much about looking for a new job? Do you think things are going pretty well for you here?

Amanda: [Laughs] I'm not looking for a job, don't worry. Things are OK.

Manager: But just "OK". What if we had a job opening...would you tell your friends about it? Would you encourage them to apply?

Amanda: Yes, definitely. The benefits are great here, the people are good to work with. I'd recommend it.

Manager: How about the issue of communication? Happy with the level of communication on the team or can we be doing better?

Amanda: Well, I don't want to be negative but I don't think we really know what's going on around here. It seems like projects pop-up with no notice, and we're only told about our specific area...we never see the big picture.

Manager: What about learning and training? How do you feel things are going in this area?

Amanda: Can't complain about that. Between the online courses, tuition reimbursement and new software training, I think we have plenty. Maybe just not enough time to take advantage of all of it.

Manager: OK. How about the area of recognition? Do you feel the company is recognizing your accomplishments?

Amanda: I'm not looking for that. I mean getting a thank you is always nice. I have wondered why nobody from our department ever gets recognized in the President's letter.

Manager: OK, last question. How do you feel about the future of the company? How confident are you that we can accomplish our goals?

Amanda: I don't even know what the company's goals are. I just focus on what I need to do each day and figure the rest will take care of itself.

Manager: I understand. Well, we'll be trying to make improvements in a lot of these areas and we'll work as a team to brainstorm some things we can do. Thanks again for letting me know how you feel about all of this.

Notice that the manager isn't trying to solve Amanda's issues or have a big debate about them. The purpose of a stay interview is to just gather information. You can come back later to discuss possible remedies.

CHAPTER 7:
STEP TWO, SHARE
THE RESULTS

After taking the time to conduct your engagement survey, you then need to share-out the results in a team meeting.

In fact, the reason why so many employees are cynical about employee surveys is because they take up a lot of time and nothing ever seems to come from them. Either they never hear another peep or maybe they get a meeting from HR about it and then it goes into a black hole.

In leading my various companies, I would always conduct a survey and share the results every six months. In fact, I would always show two slides in the survey results meeting.

The first slide would just show the *averages* for all the questions. (Important: you never want to show individual results in a team meeting. It's supposed to be anonymous, remember?!)

My first slide for the team meeting would look like:

---

1. I am extremely satisfied working at Company X. = 3.5

2. I rarely think about finding a new job in a different company. = 3.8

3. I would recommend Company X to my friends as a great place to work. = 4.0

4. There is frequent, two-way communication at Company X. = 3.2

5. Company X provides me with sufficient opportunities for learning and development. = 3.8

6. I feel appreciated at work. = 3.9

7. I am confident that Company X has a bright future. = 2.3

The second slide would show a graph depicting the results over time. Are we getting better or worse? Did we improve on the items we focused on?

The key is to facilitate a discussion about the results (emphasis on *facilitate*, don't be the one doing all the talking and don't be defensive).

Sharing your survey results publicly, even if the scores are low, shows that you are serious about the engagement process. You'll earn respect and trust just by being transparent with the team's current engagement level.

In this team meeting, play the role of the facilitator and get people talking with key questions.

"What do you think about our scores?"

"Which questions and scores are standing out to you?"

"Are you surprised at how low/high the score on question #X is?"

"What are some ideas that could improve communication on our team?"

"What would have to change in order for all of you to tell your friends this is a great place to work?"

Ideally, you only want to pick one or two items to focus on for improvement. If you are doing a survey every six months or more frequently than that, I'd suggest just pick one item. If you are only doing the survey annually, you can pick two items.

And be realistic about how much improvement you can see in each survey cycle. Most leaders can improve their engagement score, and the score of their number one focus area, by about five to ten percent a year. So if you're overall engagement score comes back as a 3.0, a realistic goal would be to try to get it up to a 3.3 the next time you do the survey.

Remember, your job in the action planning meeting is to facilitate and listen. Don't judge their answers or be dismissive.

Depending on your current level of team-trust and your colleagues experience with open communication, you might get a whole flip chart of new ideas, or you might hear crickets.

Crickets are OK. Remember, your job is to ask and listen. If they don't want to share, you can't force them. As they learn over time that you are serious about wanting to improve engagement, they'll learn to open up.

CHAPTER 8:
STEP THREE, A
RHYTHM OF
COMMUNICATION

Communication is so critical because it forms the backbone for all other engagement efforts. To influence Growth, Recognition and Trust you must use communication.

I've learned as a leader—even a leader with some success creating highly engaged teams—you must strive to over communicate, and be OK that team members will still say you aren't communicating enough.

Over and over again I encounter frustrated CEOs who rattle off the numerous ways they "communicate" from town hall meetings, to company newsletters, to strategic plans and yet it's never enough. And usually, it's a lot of one-way broadcasting of information.

The key is to create a *system* of *two-way* communication. You need a schedule of consistent communication touch points.

ANNUALLY: Each year spend half a day or a full day with your team making sure they know what the company's goals are for the year, and how your department and their individual goals align with the company goals. The idea is to create a "line of sight" between what they do every day, and what the company is trying to achieve.

Remember, if you just lecture your team they won't remember it. Make it a discussion. Have them suggest what their annual goals should be. Have everyone create a cheat sheet that can be photocopied and pinned up on their cubicle wall, or perhaps the team can create a poster that gets displayed in a common area.

QUARTERLY: Reviewing goals and key metrics annually isn't enough; too much time passes without reminders, reinforcement and adjustments. Too many new hires have come on board who won't have alignment to your ultimate goals. Think of how American football games are broken into four quarters—the plays that are called in the fourth quarter are often very different than the ones called in the beginning of the game.

Similar to your annual meeting, quarterly meetings should be a time to pause and review progress against annual objectives, and set objectives for the quarter. In other words, break the big annual goals down into quarterly actions.

Ideally, spend some time doing team building each quarter too. It's important to acknowledge great effort and accomplishments and enable team members to have some fun. I would do meetings in the morning and then take my team out in the afternoon to the movies, or for bowling, or to a baseball game. If you have little or no budget, even just doing a pizza party in the conference room can be a nice break from the daily routine.

WEEKLY: Meet one-on-one with each direct report for 15-30 minutes. This is vital. This gives you a few minutes of personal time so you can know about any major things going on in their life (e.g., "So, how was your weekend?") and then enables you to review progress from the prior week, and review priorities for the current week. I always end these meetings with the same question, "What specifically do you need from me this week?"

I would always stack these up and do them all in a row on Monday morning. I'd usually review my to do lists and calendar with my admin first thing on Monday morning, but by 10am I'd be doing my one-on-ones. By noon or early afternoon they'd be done and I'd feel good that everyone was crystal clear on their weekly goals and that they all had a chance to ask for advice or help if needed.

If you have four direct reports these one-on-one meetings would take between one to two hours of your day. If you have ten direct reports it would take from 2.5 to five hours each Monday. It sounds like a big investment of time, but will actually save time by eliminating problems down the road and increasing engagement.

As you can guess, my Mondays are pretty packed with internal meetings. There is time for a round of return phone calls and emails, but little else. The truth is that doing Monday meetings right means you rarely need to do internal meetings the rest of the week.

Also, do a full-team meeting each week for 30-60 minutes. I would typically do these at 5pm each Monday. The purpose was to review key metrics and give each person "peripheral vision" as to what else was going on in the department. In other words, each person would report out to their fellow team members. It's a great way to ensure accountability. ("Joe, you mentioned last Monday that you were wrapping up the Marketing Plan for the Widget Launch, but you didn't mention it this week. How's that going?")

I would use the Monday full-team meetings to review my "data dashboard." As CEO, this would primarily consist of revenue recognition updates, key project deadlines, etc. Again, these were updated weekly by the team members themselves and reported out for all to see.

Here are some other ways you can improve your personal communication skills on a daily basis.

Idea #1) Practice active listening. When other people are talking to you, *truly listen*. Most people are too busy thinking about what they want to say next, or are mentally attacking the position. Just listen. And then, paraphrase back what you heard just to make sure you got it right, and to make sure the other person knows you were listening.

Idea #2) Use a variety of communication tactics. Realize that people have different preferred communication styles. It's easy and efficient to rely on management-by-email, but it's also cold and subject to miscommunication. Mix it up. Send emails, call people on the phone, talk over a cup of coffee, or send out an old fashioned paper memo if you really want to get noticed.

Idea #3) Specify "what" not "how". Avoid micromanaging by being crystal clear with your desired goals, but leave it up to your direct report to figure out how best to accomplish it. I usually just specify the goal and conclude with, "Let me know if you need any help or advice."

Idea #4) Call people out. In group meetings don't just ask for questions and opinions; many good, smart people become quiet in group settings. Get in the habit of specifically calling people out (e.g., "Kevin, what do you think about this idea?" or "Paige, what do you like about this idea and what do you think could go wrong?")

Idea #5) Make other people solve the problems. People who've worked with me before know my infamous trick of making the person who has a suggestion also be the one to find a solution. "Owen, you're right that we should do more team building events around here. Why don't you pick two people to help you come up with ideas for next month?"

Idea #6) Invite people from other departments to come in for "lunch and learns" (e.g., HR, IT, Sales, etc.). You can buy the team pizza, or just invite people to bring their lunch to the conference room, and have your guest speaker come in to talk about the latest developments in their department and to take questions.

Idea #7) If you have a big team, use an old fashioned anonymous suggestion box. Leave it in the lunchroom or on your assistant's desk. Once a month open it up, post all suggestions on a bulletin board (again, transparency earns respect and trust), and take action on the ideas.

Idea #8) Use "parallel thinking" in meetings where you invite everyone to come up with the risks, the benefits and key steps to implement. This way it's a team decision or the team's project, and it's not pitting one person against another.

A final reminder: remember these two things. First, you can never communicate too much. Second, put a focus on *two-way* communication, not just broadcasting information.

CHAPTER 9:
STEP FOUR,
GROWTH

When it comes to Growth, **people need to feel that they are advancing towards their career objectives and are learning new things**. They need to feel that their manager cares about their growth and advancement.

For each direct report, you should schedule a one-on-one "career meeting" with them (repeat this meeting every six months). The goal is simply to help them to identify their career goals and what they need to achieve them.

- **What are their career goals for the current year?** In the next three to five years?

- **Can those goals be accomplished within your department?** Within the company?

- **What knowledge, skills and attitudes are required for their current position?** What about for their future desired position?

When thinking about career development and skill building options, don't just think of traditional training programs. Consider other low-cost options that might actually be more valuable. These include:

A Coach—someone outside the company, that can provide objective and private advice.

A Mentor—someone inside the company, perhaps in a different department or someone who currently holds the position the employee would one day like to obtain.

Developmental Projects—assign them to teams where, although they might not be a key contributor, they can be exposed to new areas and meet new people.

Job Rotations—whether for a day, a week, or a month, arrange for your team member to swap jobs with someone in another department. Again, the goal isn't that they'd master the new job, but rather that they gain exposure to new areas and people.

Ultimately you want to create a culture that fosters growth among all team members. Knowing what their goals are, and what skills they need to develop will help you to provide assistance along the way.

Chapter 10:
Step Five,
Recognition

Employees need to feel appreciated. For a very few, this results from a big bonus check or winning a spot in the President's Club. But for most people, appreciation comes from the more routine actions of their manager, on a day to day basis.

You need to make sure you are taking the time to say thank you and to acknowledge the accomplishments of your team members. As long as it's deserved, you can't say "good job" too much.

There are many forms of appreciation that require little to no money:

Say thank you—two simple words that have an immediate impact. Saying it in front of others will magnify its impact.

Write thank you—written thank you notes have become a lost art. The value of a "thank you" is often related to the amount of time it takes to deliver. While jotting off a quick email is better than nothing, taking the time to hand write a note will become a prized memento, often tacked to the cubicle wall for years to come.

Remember Doug Conant, from our Campbell Soup case study? Doug would end each day by hand writing 20 notes to employees and partners. He estimates that he wrote 30,000 notes in his time at Campbell's! Think about Doug the next time you think you are too busy to write a thank you note. Here he is, a Fortune 500 CEO tasked with saving an iconic company from bankruptcy. It's 6pm or later in the day—you know he has more emails to respond to, more reports to read, more phone calls to return—but he stops all that to write out his 20 notes.

Praise the employee to others—consider sending an email to your boss about the accomplishment of a team member, and cc: them on the message. Alternatively, send a note to their spouse letting them know how valuable they are to the success of your team.

Buy lunch—sometimes the gift of time has a dramatic effect. Take someone out to lunch (it doesn't have to be fancy) as a way to acknowledge their good work and to build a tighter bond.

Get in the habit of a three part "thank you". This consists of (1) say thanks, (2) specifically mention the behavior or achievement and (3) explain what it means to the company or how it aligns with your strategic priorities. For example:

"Good morning, everyone. Before we start this meeting I just wanted to publicly say, 'Thanks, Carlos, for all the overtime you've been putting in lately.' Because of his willingness to give some extra hours we were able to finish the Acme project and book the revenue this month. And because of that, we'll hit our stretch goal of 20% growth on the year."

25 Low Cost Ways to Thank Colleagues

1. A sincere word of thanks is very effective.

2. Post a thank-you note on the person's door.

3. Throw a pizza party or cake party in the person's honor.

4. Create a simple "ABCD" card that is given when someone goes "Above and Beyond the Call of Duty."

5. Write about colleagues in a company-wide email message.

6. Give a long lunch, an extra break, or comp time.

7. Honor colleagues at the start of the next staff meeting (or recognize someone at the start of every staff meeting).

8. In the lobby, post a "thank you" sign with the person's name on it.

9. Give colleagues flowers, a book, or some other small gift.

10. Invite colleagues to a one-on-one lunch.

11. Give them a card with lottery tickets inside.

12. Give them a card with movie tickets inside, or better yet, take them to a matinee.

13. Give them a card with a Starbucks gift certificate.

14. Have the entire team sign a framed photo or certificate of appreciation.

15. Arrange for a boss several levels up to stop by to say thanks.

16. Send a thank-you note or gift basket to the person's spouse.

17. Arrange to have the person's car washed.

18. Arrange to have the person's home cleaned.

19. Let people bring their pets to work.

20. Buy a dozen donuts and announce to the department that they are in the honorees' office, and people should stop by to say hi and get one.

21. Feature colleagues in the company newsletter.

22. Pick an unusual or funny object and place it on the person's desk for a week.

23. Have the entire team honor the person with a standing ovation at the start of the next staff meeting.

24. Pay for their spouse to accompany the employee on a business trip.

25. Temporarily name a conference room after the honored employee; put their picture on the wall.

Finally, an important way to make people feel appreciated is to get them involved. Ask for their opinion on various issues. It doesn't mean you need to accept every idea they have, but they'll appreciate it as long as you listen.

SAD FACT

Only 10% of adults say thank you
to a colleague each day.

Only 7% express gratitude to a boss.

(Source: Gratitude Survey,
by Janice Kaplan, John Templeton Foundation, 2012)

CHAPTER 11: STEP SIX, TRUST

When it comes to Trust, your employees need to both trust that their leaders are honest and ethical, but also that they can trust that their leaders will get them to the Promised Land (whatever big, hairy audacious goal your company has).

When it comes to being honest and ethical one would think that it isn't something that needs to be taught. You'd think almost everyone acts ethically. Unfortunately, in my own experience I've encountered many executives who, for whatever reason, can't fully be trusted.

Here are some basic reminders:

Your words and deeds must match. So simple but so easy to trip on. I've known "leaders" who promised bonuses but gave pies instead, who promised benefits wouldn't change and then they did, who promised to meet one-on-one but never fit it into their schedule, who promised the office would get a fresh coat of paint but it never occurred, and on and on and on.

In most of these cases I think these were good people who got caught up in the moment, or perhaps found it easier to offer good news than reality. Regardless, when they didn't deliver on what they said they would they were immediately judged to be not trustworthy by their followers. Be careful what you say, and make sure to keep your promises.

Be transparent; share the bad news along with the good. Many leaders believe that it is their job to be actors whose job it is to rally the troops and keep morale high. But leaders can become "liars" through omission. While you don't want to dwell on the negative, you gain trust by being transparent and giving people the information they need to make their own judgments.

Acknowledge mistakes. Nobody is perfect, including leaders. But when you make a mistake you need to acknowledge it. This simple act will erase any ill will generated by the shortcoming.

In addition to being honest, you need to instill confidence in the future; your team needs to "trust" that you can take them to your stated objectives.

> *"It is the job of leaders to eliminate uncertainty."*
> **--Colin Powell**

To build confidence in the future you must, **first, define your future.** While it can be helpful to have inspirational but vague vision statements, the most powerful thing a leader can do is to develop a big, hairy audacious goal, or BHAG (pronounced bee-hag). This is the term coined by management guru Jim Collins. It's a specific goal, set three to ten years in the future, with perhaps only a 50/50 chance of being accomplished.

KEY POINT

A BHAG is an effective way to set and communicate
a medium-term goal that will focus attention
and unify effort throughout your organization.

Second, give your BHAG a short, catchy, memorable name. A future vision is meaningless if nobody can remember what it is. Here are some samples I've collected from various companies.

- Ansell: "2x in 3y" (double revenues within 3 years)

- BioRad: "BIG!" ($5 Billion in Sales, Independent, and Global)

- SAP: "20 by 2015" (20 Billion Euros by the year 2015)

- Coca-Cola: "2020 Vision" (Double revenue by the year 2020)

- Citizens & Northern Bank: 20/20—$20 share price and $20 million in net profits

Now you might be saying, "Kevin, I'm a grunt manager, not the CEO. I can't control our company's strategic goals or 'BHAG'."

Fair enough, but you can take their strategic vision and make it catchy for your team. Your direct reports' engagement is tied to you more than the company.

Let's have some fun with this. I'm going to do a Google search on "strategic plan" and see what comes up, and then we'll see if we can make other people's strategic plans catchy.

OK, here's one from a power company in India. Sifting out the blah, blah, blah and we read:

The Strategic Plan covers grid-interactive power generation from the main renewable energy sources solar, wind, biomass and small hydro power... leading to total renewable power generation capacity of about 73,000 MW by 2022. This capacity will comprise of

20,000 MW from solar power under the National Solar Mission and the remaining 30,000 MW from other renewable energy sources mainly wind, small hydro and biomass power.

So basically they have a plan to build up their renewable power sources by the year 2022 (i.e., in 10 years). How can we make this catchy and memorable for rank and file employees? How about:

- "73 in 10" meaning 73 megawatts of renewable power in 10 years.

- Or, "73 by 22" referencing the year 2022.

Notice that we're emphasizing the specific goal, and the specific year to reach it by.

Also, if the company plan just seems too remote, feel free to create a BHAG for your team.

For example, let's say you lead a small accounting team, inside a global software mega-company. Their goal is to double revenue in a decade, largely through acquisitions. Your team of finance folks might see the "line of sight" between what they do and what the company is trying to achieve. Your job is to show them how their daily activities support the overall mission. Their efforts to reduce tax exposure leads to more profit that can be used for acquisitions. Their speedy work on due diligence means acquisitions are more likely to close and more can be completed in the time allotted. You could come up with your own team goal and catchy phrase.

Lastly, don't forget to communicate your BHAG often.

Using the "73 by 22" phrase we came up with, you could give everyone a postcard with that statement and inspirational imagery.

- You could hang posters throughout the office displaying "73 by 22."

- You could end every single team memo or newsletter with "Remember 73 by 22!"

- You could call out people randomly in your meetings and ask them what your goal is and give them a small prize if they can recite it.

Nobody can feel engaged if they are distrustful of leadership and scared of the future. You need to earn trust daily, through your words and your deeds.

Chapter 12: Eight Weeks to Engagement! (or, Putting It All Together)

I've shown you how you can drive massive commitment and engagement in only six steps, but we covered a lot of ground quickly. Here's how to actually execute the plan.

DAY ONE: Read and Commit

Read this book and commit to giving it a try. You will be surprised at how quickly the tips become habits and how quickly your team will get engaged.

WEEK ONE: Build the Survey

Go to an online survey website like surveymonkey.com and sign-up for a free account. Type in the survey questions I provided in Chapter Five.

WEEK TWO: Measure It

Send the link to the survey to all of your direct reports and explain that it's super short and will help you to make it a better place to work. If a survey isn't your style, just type up the questions on a sheet of paper and ask people to anonymously fill it out and stick it in a big envelope or suggestion box. Or simpler still, just have a heartfelt engagement conversation—a "stay interview"—with your team members and use my questions as a guide.

WEEK THREE: Analyze Results

Use the online survey software to run simple reports. Remember, you're looking for overall averages, not individual responses.

Create a couple slides or copy the results onto a single sheet of paper.

WEEK FOUR: Share and Discuss the Results

Call a team meeting and share the results of the survey. Don't lecture, just facilitate. What does your team think of the results? What's going best? What area needs the most work?

At this point, a month into the process, your direct reports will *feel* like engagement is on your mind, and is a priority.

WEEK FIVE: Establish a Rhythm of Communication

This is a big week. Send out calendar invites for all your one-on-one meetings as well as your team meetings. Go ahead and schedule a whole year's worth. That way people will have plenty of notice for the meetings and will see that you're committed and it's not just a fad.

Expect dissent and challenge on this step. Handle objections by letting people know that the meetings will be brief and productive and will lead to fewer ad hoc "got a minute" meetings. They'll feel more in the loop with what is going on with everyone on the team, and you'll be doing your best to share news from other areas of the company.

After executing this step, your team members will *feel* better informed, that they have a chance to give input, and they'll *feel* more aligned to the overall goals of the organization.

WEEK SIX: Hold Career Meetings

This is the week when you'll want to schedule one-on-one career exploration meetings with each direct report. You can probably get each meeting done in 30 minutes, but if you have the time, it might be nice to do it for an hour over lunch or a cup of coffee. If you have 10 direct reports this means you'll be scheduling 5 to 10 hours of meetings. If you find that you can't fit them all into one week, spreading them out over the month is fine too.

Remember that your goal isn't to have all the answers or to guarantee each person that they will achieve their goal. Just make sure they are sharing what their career path plans are, and have an honest discussion about what knowledge, skills and attitudes they need to acquire in order to get there.

Begin to brainstorm ways to close the gap, but again, don't expect to have it all figured out in one meeting. The goal is just to make you aware of what they need so you can provide it as needed in the months or years ahead.

Your direct reports will begin to *feel* that they will continue to learn and to develop, and they will know that you are open to their career needs.

WEEK SEVEN: Develop Recognition Habits

Making people feel appreciated shouldn't just happen during this one week, but it's a good time to start the development of *daily* habits.

Catch team members doing good things and thank them for it. Start every team meeting by acknowledging the good work of an individual, or the accomplishments of your entire team. End each day with a written thank you note. Develop the mindset of appreciation.

Your team members will *feel* more appreciated.

WEEK EIGHT: Build Trust & Confidence

Similar to week seven, building trust and confidence in the future isn't limited to a single week. But this is the week that you can be mindful of it.

Review your company's strategic plan, or BHAG, and think about ways you can reinforce it with your team. Talk to team members about whether or not they feel they know where the company is going in the years ahead. Make sure everybody is crystal clear when it comes to your company's and your team's goals. If your company doesn't already have a memorable phrase that encapsulates goals, work with your team to create one.

Your team members will *feel* more confident in the direction of the company and in your leadership to take them there.

IN SIX MONTHS: Repeat Survey

After your initial 8-week process, you should be mindful daily of creating an environment that ritualizes two-way communication, and fosters growth, recognition and trust.

Repeat the survey or stay-interview process every six months. There will always be a "lowest score", even when all scores are good. So focus on your one area of weakness and tackle it head on.

Additionally, repeat the one-on-one career meetings every six months. These meetings will make sure your direct reports feel that they are advancing and that you are committed to their success.

While your team members may initially be skeptical of your new engagement efforts, after six months of time they'll realize that this is the new normal. Soon, their skepticism will fade and they will *feel* engaged.

CHAPTER 13:
Q&A

Whenever I do a keynote speech, workshop or webinar there are always many questions from participants. Here are some of the more common ones.

Question: Everyone is just too busy to be doing engagement stuff—where do you find the time?

Engagement done right requires very little time. For individual managers, driving growth requires a 30-minute coffee meeting every six months. Driving recognition means they might spend the first 30-seconds of every meeting acknowledging someone in the room, or 60-seconds at the end of each day to write one thank you note. Creating a BHAG and instilling confidence in the future might require a pizza-lunch to create, or if the future mission is already crystal clear it just takes repetition, not time.

When it comes to the engagement survey, if you do them twice a year (or annually which is better than not at all), each employee would probably spend 60 seconds to 2 minutes completing the survey, and reviewing the results as a team would require one-hour every six months.

The most important thing is to realize that when you have unlocked discretionary effort, you will get massive gains in productivity. People will do more work, with a higher quality, in less time than ever before. You'll spend less time fixing things, taking corrective action, firing people, recruiting new people. Engagement is a time saver, not a time waster.

Question: Does engagement vary by age? Or, are the Millennials less engaged than other generations?

Younger workers, and older workers, tend to be slightly more engaged. If you looked at a graph it would look like a "U" where the mid-career professionals are least engaged. Nobody knows why for sure, but rather than this being some kind of generational trait, I think it just reflects where we are in our career.

My guess is that newer workers are all green and excited to be joining the workforce and fighting to make their mark on the world. The oldest workers are also the ones more advanced in their career and probably a little closer to senior leadership. In most companies, the closer you are to the CEO the more engaged you are. If you're a

40 something year old professional with a manager or director title and a bunch of people to manage, you might be slightly less engaged than the other camps.

Question: Does engagement vary by type of work?

Yes, but the difference is small; all groups are primarily not engaged. For example, 2012 Gallup research showed that 36% of executives are engaged versus only 24% engagement for manufacturing workers. So, yes, grinding away on the factory floor seems to be less engaging than that white collar office job. But the big picture is the same, the vast majority of workers are not engaged.

Question: Does engagement vary by gender?

Same answer as above. Yes, women tend to be slightly more engaged than men (33% vs. 28%) but in both groups most people are not engaged.

Question: How can I "sell" my boss on engagement?

I think C-level executives need to hear about the business results. I believe that all people make decisions based on emotion, but they use logic to justify it. So, sharing case studies like the one with Doug Conant at Campbell Soup will emotionally demonstrate that other high level leaders are getting hard business results from this "soft" engagement stuff. It never hurts to share the research, too (see Appendix C at end of the book).

Also, whenever selling anything "new" a good strategy is to just sell a "pilot". Try to get permission to roll-out an engagement survey and training to one team, or one department or one location. Show before and after engagement results and see if they correlate to performance gains.

CHAPTER 14: CONCLUSION

If you want to be an engaging leader just to help your company's bottom line, you are likely to fail. **Despite our best intention to be leaders of people, we usually become managers of tasks and projects**; we get pushed around by the never ending to do list, the torrent of email messages, and overlapping calendar appointments.

To make engagement a daily priority, focus less on the profit reason and more on the people reason. What you do as a boss impacts lives outside of the office.

Try this exercise: choose a valuable member of your team. Pick someone who is important to your team's success, and picture her in your mind. (If you don't have any direct reports you can still play along. Just pick someone on your team that is important to you.)

Do you see this valued person? Good. Now picture her spouse or significant other. Picture her kids if she has any.

Now realize that even though you aren't a doctor, what you say to this person impacts her health.

You aren't a teacher, but what you do as a boss impacts how her kids behave in school.

You aren't a marriage counselor, but your behavior as a leader impacts whether she goes home and kisses her husband, or goes home and argues with him.

Feel this extraordinary influence you have over individuals and their families. *This is why you need to be a true leader*.

First and foremost we need *you* to be engaged. It has to start with you. And it's what you need to be not just for your company, but for your own family and friends.

Then, you need to be mindful of engagement on a daily basis. Create habits for Communication, Growth, Recognition and Trust, so your entire team can experience the benefits of full engagement.

Good luck!

Appendix A: Book Club Discussion Questions

Many companies have formed books clubs or discussion groups around *Employee Engagement 2.0*. The questions below can be used to facilitate a conversation about how the ideas in the book can be used to increase engagement in your own organization.

1. What is the difference between employee satisfaction, employee happiness, and employee engagement?

2. If everyone on your team was giving discretionary effort—going above and beyond what was required of their job—what impact would it make on your team? For the company?

3. Describe a time when your emotions from work spilled over to your personal life, and crossed over to friends or family members.

4. Think of a time when you worked for a great boss, and a time when you worked for a bad boss. What were the traits of each (i.e., what about them made them great or bad)?

5. Do the four drivers of engagement seem to match up with your own experience, and the list of traits of a great boss?

6. What are some ways to improve two-way communication on your team?

7. How can you stimulate feelings of growth and development, without the use of traditional training classes?

8. What are some no-cost or low-cost ways to show appreciation for their efforts or their achievements?

9. How does "Trust" relate to the future?

10. What is your company's long-term objectives and strategic plan? How can you summarize it and make it easy to remember?

APPENDIX B: ENGAGEMENT AND BUSINESS RESULTS

I maintain a master list of research findings that show a correlation between employee engagement and:

- Service
- Sales
- Quality
- Safety
- Retention
- Sales, Profit and Total Shareholder Returns
- Role of Front-Line Managers
- Causation and Linkage

For an always up-to-date list of employee engagement research visit:

http://kevinkruse.com/employee-engagement-research-master-list-of-29-studies/

If you would like to suggest a research report to be included in my list, please email info@kevinkruse.com.

New from Kevin Kruse!

The only book written specifically to teach
INDIVIDUAL EMPLOYEES
how to be accountable for their own engagement

In *Employee Engagement for Everyone*, individual employees learn how to partner with their supervisors to become fully engaged.

Your employees will discover:

- The 4 drivers of happiness and engagement at work

- Their own personal engagement style

- 60+ specific actions they can take to drive their own engagement, and the engagement of those around them

- How to deal with a "Debbie Downer" in the office

- The power of "5 Daily Engagement Questions"

4 Keys to Happiness and Fulfillment at Work

Employee Engagement for Everyone

New York Times Bestselling Author
Kevin Kruse

Discover Your Personal Engagement Profile

"We give this book to all our new employees as part of their orientation process."
--Ian Kelly, CEO, Red Nucleus, #1 Best Place to Work in NJ

Workshop or Keynote

Imagine dramatically increasing employee engagement throughout your organization, by teaching your senior leaders the keys to unlocking emotional commitment.

"Leading for Employee Engagement with Kevin Kruse"

Kevin Kruse speaks around the world at executive retreats, leadership meetings and association conferences. Based on his *New York Times* bestseller, *We*, and *Employee Engagement 2.0*, Kevin shares the surprising findings from a massive study of 10 million workers in 150 countries, along with his own experiences as a former "Best Place to Work" award-winning CEO.

Your team will learn why engagement is critical to your company's success, and how they can unleash engagement on their own teams.

"Kevin woke up the crowd in a very tough time slot... got them engaged and laughing. He gave ideas that could be implemented right away and his ending left everyone inspired."
--Elliot Clark, CEO, SharedXpertise

To invite Kevin to speak at your next event call

e-mail info@kevinkruse.com
or call 267-756-7089.

ABOUT
KEVIN KRUSE

Kevin Kruse is globally recognized as a leading expert in employee engagement and leadership. He is a *New York Times*, *Wall Street Journal*, and *USA Today* bestselling author, and *Forbes* columnist.

In pursuit of the American Dream, Kevin Kruse started his first company when he was just 22 years old. He worked around the clock, literally living out of his one-room office and showering each day at the YMCA, before giving up a year later deeply in debt.

But after discovering the power of Wholehearted Leadership and employee engagement, Kevin went on to build and sell several, multimillion dollar technology companies, winning both Inc. 500 and Best Place to Work awards along the way.

Website: www.KevinKruse.com.

LinkedIn: http://www.linkedin.com/in/kevinkruse67